Still Life

Still Life

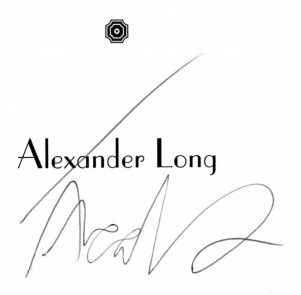

Alexander Long

White Pine Press Poetry Prize, Volume 16

White Pine Press / Buffalo, New York

White Pine Press
P.O. Box 236
Buffalo, New York 14201
www.whitepine.org

Publication of this book was made possible, in part, with
public funds from the New York State Council on the Arts,
a State Agency.

State of the Arts

NYSCA

ACKNOWLEDGMENTS (continued on page 114)

Thank you to editors of the following publications in which some of these poems first
appeared, sometimes in different versions:

AGNI: "Style in Slow Motion"
The American Poetry Review: "Ars Poetica #17," "Goodbye in Slow Motion with Those
Trees Waving Back"
Arroyo Poetry Journal: "Still Life with Frederick Douglass Learning the Alphabet,
Stopping for a Moment at O," "Still Life with Paul Celan by the Seine"
Big Toe Review: "Still Life without History," "Still Life with a Grain of Rice," "Still
Life with Sisyphus Smiling"
Boxcar Poetry Review: "Still Life with the Atlantic Ocean and Nina Simone as
Soundtrack"
Callaloo: "Malcolm X Transcribing the Dictionary in Slow Motion"
Connotation Press: An Online Artifact: "Spilt Coffee in Slow Motion," "Still Life with
Geraniums"
The Offending Adam: "Still Life with Lenny Bruce in Jail," "Prayer #34," "Still Life
with Issa at the Gates"
Three Candles Journal: "Still Life with Suicide II: with Hendrix and Vallejo Folding
Their Cards and Showing Their Losses"
Third Coast: "Still Life with Kafka Checking His Watch, Missing His Train"
The Toledo Review: "Koi Pond in Slow Motion"
Unsplendid: "Still Life with Addict"
Zone 3: "Still Life with Abraham Lincoln, Twenty-Three Years before the Confederacy
Shot Him, a Hundred Years before the Nazis Tried to Prove Him Wrong"

Cover Photo: Josef Koudelka
Cover Design: Elaine LaMattina

First Edition
ISBN: 978-1-935210-29-0
Printed and bound in the United States of America.
Library of Congress Control Number: 2011931990

In memory of Morton Marcus & Larry Levis

Table of Contents

IV

V

There's stillness in their motion & motion in their stillness.

—Larry Levis

Koi Pond in Slow Motion

They move under ice as thin as a bible's paper.

I don't dare crack it because they seem
Not to move at all.
                    Isn't this how it is, after all,

Come December? Wanting to shut down
For awhile and glide a glacial pace, slow

Work and slower heart and slowest
Of loves not sliding by, maybe, until April

Slips inside the lungs, when the koi's eyes
Widen like irises and their tails wave

Like laundry on the line, their gills healthy gashes
Letting in then out the ice as thin as a bible's

Paper that's melted so we can stare at their sway

And forget, awhile, our own slipping away
And waving, even while it's happening

To each of us this very,
                    and every, moment.

I

Still Life without History

I offer it up because I can.
I am an American.

But why can't I make out a single word of what this *it* is,

Why do I feel more lost than a t-shirt
Of Ernesto Guevara I saw hanging

In a boutique off Aldstadter Ring, where Kafka
Snuck a smoke before Hitler and Stalin

Tried to erase the names of the streets?

Praha loosely translates into threshold,

And those who were there are here now
In something I can't compose, whose motif

Is what they have lost,

This *it* I'm not permitted touch
But want.

Some sing to the star that burns
The first snow no one can mark.

Others listen a long time

For a deeper translation that knits itself
Into the stubborn weeds along a riverbank

Where an elderly couple gather water
As snow fills the space of the long yield

Still others call hope

Until History appears on its chestnut mare,
Dressed in the state-issued drab-green coat and hat,

Chewing an unlit cigar, filing its report:

What they hear is History itself, a joke that no one gets—
Even the teller, the one who cries with laughter.

He tells the joke over and over and over

Until the listeners catch on that the joke is
There is no joke, but only moments

Of stars shining, brief flickers to sing to.

Until the joke, in fact, becomes a song the state accommodates,
Something as forgettable as water music,

As water I can't touch.

What does it feel like to sing air fissioned
By an accident called History?

How do you compose water
Sliding through your hands, fire sung to,

A body here, a song there,

There, in the mouth of a schoolgirl
In a city once called Pripyat, a village once called Raduga:

It's December, 1989, and she taps her foot on the cracked
    asphalt,
Bored singing to herself.

She waits for the sign to hoist the flag,

Only there's no one to give the sign,
Nor was a flag ever agreed upon.

Her feet are numb and her nose runs,

Yet she doesn't know when to give up,
When to raise the flag that doesn't exist

Yet. And all I see in this moment
Is that there's no one to call her back

To the chores of pickling cucumbers, no one to punish
Her for skipping the piano lesson

For which her father saved and saved;
No cucumbers, no piano, no teacher, no music.

How is that? That can't be, can it?

I mean, I hear something.

Still Life with Abraham Lincoln, Twenty-Three Years before the Confederacy Shot Him, a Hundred Years before the Nazis Tried to Prove Him Wrong

Or let's say we have no choice.

Or pick a century.

Let's say we're in a line that stretches a hundred train cars long.

It's August in Bergen-Belsen, Gettysburg, Springfield.

Or it's the night before
He gets married, and after eighteen months of separation,
    Lincoln

Comes to the exact place Mary Todd instructs him.

Before he can breathe no, his soul smolders.

                    * * *

Now, let's say, he understands the fear and the rapture
Of tigers sprung from the cages of P. T. Barnum.

Let's say, in this moment, Lincoln resigns
Himself fully to pleasure, forsaking no one,

Then thinks better of it.

After all, a man with scruples will not simply fuck
And walk away. This is why Davis will take him down,

And know he can.

But, it's still 1842, and look here,
His letters gush like Job:

"To remain as I am is impossible; I must die or be better, it
      appears to me."

His depression eclipses, say, Poe's or Plath's.

His only allies, Celan & Kafka, nod their assent.

After the fact, they've blessed him and sing with the wrens:
We came to this together, we'll finish this together.

                    * * *

He sweats on the courthouse steps. He pushes
His glasses up from the tip of his nose,

Takes them off, dabs his forehead with a handkerchief.

If you want him to run down the steps into the streets
Of what are becoming The Heartland,

Sorry, he's already thought the better of that as well.

There's nothing in his vision. Nothing

From which we want him to dream a nation
Of clouds re-flowering the South.

It doesn't matter what we want.

What he needs to know in this moment, simply
Because he's a man, is not what will happen,

But who he will not become.

Still Life with Frederick Douglass Learning the Alphabet, Stopping for a Moment at O

All you're taught about how he gave himself a name, long

After he learned who he was
Not is a myth.

And today, like yesterday, is also a myth,
And all you've learned

About all he may never know—
How old he is, how old he'll never be—

Is an image for us to curl into and fall asleep.

We have a choice now
To slowly wade into images until we find ourselves

Gasping for air, waving through all that watery light above,
To learn again how language works through images.

Let's start here:

When the language is not our own,
When it comes twirling a whip and whistling Dixie,

When our tongue slips down our throats
In some feeble, necessary attempt to keep ourselves

From throwing it all back up;

When some silver sky behind our turned-back eyes
Materializes just after we've blacked out

The whips' wish and bitch-slap across our backs;

Just before we choke on this new mother
Tongue we pray never to master;

Then, and only then, might we understand

What I heard an American historian in Warsaw
Call The Tongue of Oppressor.

"If we're lucky," he added in English, "it's ours."

Not today. Today is only an image.

Let today belong to Douglass again:

He trudges like Sisyphus through the peaks and valleys

Of M and N. His lips form
A nearly perfect circle.

If we were in the room
Hovering over his right shoulder, eavesdropping,

Adding to the myth, conscripting history
Into an image or two

We'd be more unsure than he is—

Is this his first or next-to-first breath?

Or has he only seen himself, again,
For the last time?

O, he says.

This is not a narrative of his life,

Not even an image, those tiny, essential cells
Of a narrative. This is

A moment before the present
Descends into some other unwanted language.

And even if what follows could, someday, become an image,
Or a life, what else might we have:

A gate slamming shut, no wind,
Corn stalks rustling,

A boy running toward something, a life,
Perhaps, no longer

His, chanting

O O O...?

Flash Forward with *The Amistad* before Us in the Distance

"Next," the cashier says. I step up, tissues,
Coffee, ask for Marlboro Lights. "Shit,"
The guy behind me says, "I was here first."
He wasn't. I watched him saunter in, cool,
Decked out in colors I've barely dreamed of.
"Yo, dawg," he says, "I take two blunts and twenty
Scratch offs," and pushes me aside, gently,
Almost. In this moment, I believe him:
He *was* here first. The cashier rings it up:
"$8.36." "Yo, for what? That's a good deal,"
And he laugh-coughs, looks at me, lays down a ten.
"Not you," the cashier says. "Him."
                                        The present
Has descended upon us again. Some-
One has been displaced again. This is no
Morality play, no history lesson.
This is a day like all the rest, but one
I feel more quickly than the rest. This is
The day that happens over and over
From now on.
                    I lay my ten next to his,
Look away. That's as close as we'll ever be,
I fear. I, too, have rage. He takes my ten
And leaves his for the cashier. I get my change
And stuff in a bag. "So that's how it is,"
The guy, now beside me, says. "Even now,
This day and age, a man can't even get
What he ask for? Nothing don't ever change. . . ."
I guess he went rightly on. The doors whooshed
Before me, and I walked home. I walked home.

Still Life with Sisyphus Smiling

There is but one truly serious philosophical problem and that is suicide.
—Camus

And later, Camus writes that we *must* imagine Sisyphus
Happy. The emphasis is mine
                              and is, most likely,

All wrong. Maybe Camus felt the stress falling

On *happy*, a trochee uprooting a myth, shifting

A degree or two my conscience, my tolerance for a poem

And its abyss I seem to always slide inside.

The same abyss Celan claimed was meridional, absolute,

And nonexistent,
                              a vain internalization
Of immortality, he says.

Beautiful.

But if we were to witness Celan and Kafka shake hands, how
      awkward

Would it be, and just what would they say to each other?

Would Sisyphus and his rock ever come up?

Which of them would say

For once let's have him be all at the top, singing
To the hard land and the strong sea, not
                              at the bottom muttering

Fuck. *For once, let's have him overlooking Oran,*

Morocco to his left, Sicily to his right, the Mediterranean
                                        widening

Behind his squinted, sun-flushed eyes,
                        the way a memory

Of childhood does. . . .

Which one would say *Amen, Brother?*

Neither, of course, but this is a poem that overlooks the abyss
For once, perhaps, where almost anything is possible,

Where myth shifts and Sisyphus stands
                              on Venice Beach at sunrise

While the strung-out hooker asks if she can shoot
                        up first,

You know, a little bit of ecstasy before the next
Shared fix that shames neither.

But maybe the abyss is here, in California,
                        2 p.m., November 17,
    2005,

Where Sisyphus for once feels the rush of that hour
And groans
        Oh fuck,
            and is astonished

by that ecstasy

of falling

And the pleasure it brings,

As she walks away, counting

her cash.

Still Life with Paul Celan by the Seine

—late April, 1970

Dawn sky down-soft and for the last time
Today time stops

And...? he thinks

If he smiles and runs his hand through his hair

So what

So it's a gesture withholding all that nothing

Auschwitz created

All that wordless everything inside
                              a belief

In his Seine
            the one that drifts

Grey-ice water
                toward white trees hung in his silver sky

So what if nothing isn't all that far away anymore

If today is some last day breaking
Through his hands again

He pulls two stones from his breast pocket
And presses the smooth to the jagged

Then both to his lips
                    then throat and mutters

Eternity grows older
With mild melodic antidotes

He loosens his tie
               and who needs to tell

If he's ready

To be a boy burying the throat's apple

Or a hawk waiting for release from mailed gloves

All flight passes through the throat
                     breath's slit

The glottal stop

Air and graves of air held

Throat-wide

Auschwitz's ash inside the mist of Paris again

Eternity's chirping din in the birches again

Whose every scale is held inside each cosmos
Of everything that's forbidden
                ineffable
                    and neither

Dirt-nailed and mother-tongued

Song-kept prayer-leapt throat-swept

The plumage of homage is ashen

Especially in this moment climbing inside
                              all the others

This moment
            a train
                    the next
                            an apple
                                    the next

Water herding the heart's wording

How long
        he stands there staring

At the shot moon shot through
Affable pock-marked apple

Until nothing comes
                    for the first time
                                    the first time

Again

And…?

He steps into water breathing

Still Life with Kafka Checking His Watch, Missing His Train

I wanted to start with an image of the sun
As you might have seen it, muted

By a thin sheet of ice on the windows,
The lovers inside spooning each other

On this cold morning, murmuring the harmonies
Inside solitude and honeysuckle and crepuscular

As you stroll down Altstadter Ring,
Past me waiting for the 7:40 train, and when you pass by

I look through you, though I can't entirely:

It's still 7:30 and will be for awhile.

You're still here, but I have to look through you
Because you'd want me to

Stare, instead, as long as I can at that real couple
Making the long walk, arm-in-arm,

Toward St. Vitus Cathedral; you'd want me to listen
For a very long time to their giggling

As they toss coins and miss, completely,
The green sea of the cellist's case,

At how they're so wrapped around each other,

And won't, in this moment, ever let go;

Because they make both of us utterly unaware
Of our own bodies,

Which we can't figure out. You'd dare
Me, anyone, to show what rapture might mean

Better than you have.

2. La Purisima Mission, Lompoc, California, 2004

Franz, I could tell you the stories I've heard
Of couples tossing their veils and boutonnières

Under the highway's overpass on their way to this mission.

I could tell you they do this so their families
Know they'll never show up,

Or that they'll arrive as the same person, or
As the same word:

There was sunshower and honeysuckle, and the two kids
From Lincoln, Nebraska who called themselves

Cornflower after their eyes, which were as blue
As they were silver and wide. But then,

You'd turn to me, wouldn't you, and ask what's a good way
To end it? Frightened, I'd lie:

Every day is the right day, and besides,
Who can tell that story with just one word?

And we'd sit, me packing a cigarette,
You checking your watch.

* * *

I'm sorry I lied, Franz. Let me tell one last story:
Every day is the right day.

Even if there is no music, just a bunch of wine,

Even as my friend named Frank—really—falls down
In this prolonged pause called a still life

As we make our way out of La Purisima Mission.

We were drunk that day, again, because the wine was free,
A fund-raiser for a women's shelter.

I remember wanting my friend's laughter to rise
Above any reason to laugh, any reason to fall,

Any need for a shelter.

I wanted to join him in his laughter, but
All laughter ends, even in the spirit's worst

Conditions, like when you can't name a loss,
So you call it belief or melody, until you feel

Yourself being called back to walk into a California
You see again and again and again,

But will never be able to touch:

My friend face-down in that dust, that rosa dusk
Overhead, all that laughter poured over us

Like sun on the hills of La Purisima, the same sun
That set over Prague hours ago.

I'm sorry I lied.

3. Philadelphia, New Year's Eve 2005

In Philadelphia, the calendars keep getting thinner.

I want to cry, I'm so happy. Franz, the truth is
My story contains no disaster, even as a new year takes hold.

And I stroll into it with a bottle of Ripple, and I count,
In shouts, down to one,

For I'm the only one here.

I throw stones down the tracks.

I press my hand against a grigio dawn,
This buzzing sky I once called home,

Where I'm from, where the calendars keep getting thinner.

I'll call it home, but what of that? You don't trust me
Anymore. That's why you left, isn't it?

That's why I want to put you in a poem
That seemingly never ends, and never might,

But should.

I want to make it up to you today, a little.

Home could be a salmon-hued church
With a wooden bell and iron cross,

Or a train station in Prague where I'd hoped to find
You staring at your watch and missing your train

Way back before all this started.

If I found you, would we cry with a laughter
So long and so loud that home could turn

Into a long walk with someone
You've just met?

Oh, let's cry, not because we want to, but because
We can't figure which train is yours and which is mine.

Let's get drunk one last time, again, right here,
65th & Island,

May we always miss our trains,
May someone look down upon us

And extend his hands, a cop, perhaps.

May we resume our slow and crooked walk
                                        toward our
    respective cells.

Revelation in Slow Motion

Eichmann has blue eyes

     * * *

The soul refuses to mistake identity

     * * *

He believes he is right

     * * *

As he removes a piece of flesh

     * * *

From his leather trench coat

     * * *

And knows he could do more

     * * *

Listen to history

     * * *

It's clearly happening

     * * *

It can't be tried

* * *

It can't happen fast enough

* * *

As his blue eyes bulge

* * *

As he swings in Jerusalem

* * *

It can't happen fast enough

* * *

And changes little

Two More Prayers for Depression Never to Come in Slow Motion Again

1.

May it come in a flash of negatives:

That day I'm buried shining as brightly
As a blank sheet, and that sheet withholding
All the morning-glories and hyacinths
In your ear exploding like roadside bombs
Dug and planted by St. John of the Cross,
The cross, festooned with the ivy of Hell,
Raising a white shadow over your dark
Sons and daughters like a praying lion
Rising from its rustling prayer for prey.

2.

May the flash of negatives come quickly:

The prey a gazelle sleeping now, twitching
In its dream of never running again,
The gazelle a song, a revelation,
A black light flame washing me whole again
One last time, as long as there is rhythm
To beat out of itself. May my voice turn
Back and look, like you, God, without regret,
Like a gazelle who dreams never to be
Prey, but still kneels down as the lion springs.

Prayer #34

We may say he or she
Took his or her

Life, and we will
Have to live with that.

But where? Where
Do we think

They've taken it?
May it never occur

To us to take it
Anywhere else

Than toward
This fleeting here and now

Where what we share and have
Reaches like sunlight,

Like a patient hand.
It may someday

Occur to us
To reach back

Toward our suicides
Half-smiling, half-asleep,

So we can bring
Them back.

We may regret it, finally,
But I'm telling you: reach,

Then place your lives
On their heads,

Like ashes or sunlight,
Like little hands.

Our suicides
Will answer this prayer

Only after you swear
You've seen them.

You will.
Why else reach toward them?

You will. You will
Miss them entirely,

You'll look like
You're waving,

And you will be
Embarrassed,

As if your best friend
Has ignored you.

You'll stand there
On the platform,

As the trains go
Their separate ways.

You'll busy yourself,
Pretending to fix

Your scarf
And gloves. It'll be

Cold, and the sky
A golden room.

I'll see you.
I've been there.

You'll fix your hair
And search for a smoke

And wait for the next train
You've willingly missed

Because you knew—
You did—it was him,

Her. Right there.
You swore it.

You were wrong,
Or you weren't.

So, wait.
You have to

Get home.
No choice.

The prayer?
May you never

Have to bother
With any of this.

Still Life with Suicide II: with Hendrix and Vallejo Folding Their Cards and Showing Their Losses

Me duelo ahora se explicaciones.
—Vallejo

I. Collingdale, PA 1988

For once, no one will die or be dead
Because it's not allowed anymore;

Because, for once, I say so,
And for once, almost believe it;

Because I will begin listening to this still life
Just after midnight,

While you are sleeping, reappearing
As yourself.

And what I hear is the sweetness you loved,

The way you made the Sloe Gin spill
Over your chin, the way you'd refuse

To take it as a shot.

You'd pour it to the brim
Of your father's coffee cup

And slam it,

As if there were some things
Still to be settled.

That seems right,

Hammered and righteous and right,
If only this one time, your eyes

Ablaze, belching and offering
"Pardon me, motherfucker,"

Before you resume your lecture
On Hendrix's "Fire."

Very simple, you say.

Not his best, but his most accessible.

*Two, three notes. All that style
Simplified, as if he were listening*

To all he'd lost.

                                         *   *   *

You never said that. You're dead.
You got out, and I don't know

How true that is anymore.

I almost miss you,

And I can't say that
In a poem anymore.

I'm required to give it some style,
To cut it out

Of myself and offer up it
To my next-to-last breath,

Where air is part mescaline, part music,
I'm thinking, where style is as foreign

As any pain you carved out for you
And for me,

Where loss is a parade and carnival,

And at dusk everyone joins hands
In the town square singing hymns

Laced with fire and brimstone
Without fear.

No such luck. What I say here

Has to be caught
In an image that needs to sing

Beyond explanation, pain, song;

It's got to beat itself beyond oblivion
And memory, beyond rhythm,

Itself.

A poem can't be about itself
Anymore, not when you're in it, B.

A poem can't be about the dead anymore.

II. Now

That's what's kept me up all these years,

That one thing that's kept me
Here on this page listening with you:

You keep revising yourself
With me as your muse.

It's like you're not listening.

III. Now and Forever

You motherfucker.

You'd like the crudeness of that.

You'd admire the anger.

"But, dude . . . respect," you'd say.

"You can't say 'motherfucker' in a poem
Any more than you can say 'I miss you.'"

Then, you'd take a smoke
From my packed pack without asking.

"Decorum and respect," you'd say,
Blowing the smoke in my face.

Listen: why you keep showing up
Is why I've got to slow it down,

If just for a little while,

Because I came here to talk about hope,
Just like you used to,

When you were my muse,
Before this poem started listening

To itself

And got all mixed up.

It's long past midnight, and the crickets
Are dozing off.

Now, and forever,
You're some still life,

And you will live in these lines
I've cut and burned

Inside my lungs, behind my eyes;

You will be a branch that breaks
Like a spine, a wave smashing a skull,

A flock of geese set aflame in flight,

A city walled in,
No bread, no music.

Now and forever, the world keeps its own, B.

It misses little, and has
No memory, finally,

I fear.

Leave me alone.

IV. Folding in Heaven

"Just watch," you say.

"That's Vallejo and Hendrix over there,

They just showed their cards—straight flushes
And full houses—

All the nothings luck requires—
Onto the table and called it even.

I heard Vallejo say the felt feels
Like a newborn's head.

Their cards hold our wills, man,
Hammered and righteous and right."

V. Collingdale, PA 2006

Right.

The stars are brighter this morning
Than any vision I've gotten from you.

You shot yourself.

I won't be looking
For your gravestone

Any time

Soon.

Style in Slow Motion

style: (verb) 5. To pierce with a stylet;
      (noun) 1.b. Used as a weapon of offence, for stabbing, etc.
                                        —*Oxford English Dictionary*

           —for my students

Until you taste what failure is, you will
Never sing that pain style requires.

One dark morning earlier in this life,
I felt two hooded men approaching me

In an alley. One, or both, round-housed me
From behind. I was carrying a blue

Guitar because I desired style then,
And thought it my gift to offer some.

Back then, I thought I knew what gifts were:
A voice, a song, combat boots, silver rings,

A blue guitar. But these two taught me
The true meaning of style as I came to

With asphalt in my tongue, a different
Kind of stars inside my eyes. They picked me

Up and leaned me against a wall. I spit
Blood and stones at their feet, but there were no

Poems inside that salt, nothing heroic.
One of them laughed while the other spit back

And removed a knife tucked between his boot
And shin. He brought it to his face, almost

In awe of it, as if allowed to
Hold it after a long apprenticeship.

The other laughed again, spit like his friend.
But neither said a word. This was their style:

Getting in and getting out with a slowness
Utterly fearless and without regret

Taking as much as they possibly could.
                                    And, Friends,
They did. It felt then—as it does now—

Like they had taken their own sweet, autumnal
Time knocking me down again and slashing

The flesh behind my knees with precision
And grace, like a painter, surgeon, or bear

Hunter skinning his warm kill. In this way,
They assured themselves a clean, calm exit.

But not before they removed the guitar
From its case. If they could see its clear blue

Body and turtle-shell inlay—vintage
'60 Stratocaster—they

Didn't let on until I groaned with all
The bitterness I could muster, you sons-

Uh-bitches, goddamned mother-fu . . . sons-uh. . . .
To which the one with the knife replied, what

Did you say?, the one and only direct
Question I've ever received in the slow,

Painful, confusing, and necessary
Discussion concerning itself with style.

Still Life with Lenny Bruce in Jail

All laughter is involuntary.

—L. B.

How rich you are, man.

It's what you want,
          what you can't stop

Singing:

Up in Spanish Harlem there's a rose
That's so sweet
       it grows
           up through the concrete.

I see roots as thin as veins,
          rosy veins
Blood brown reaching toward a Venus

That very well, in the palm of your hand,
            might be there.

And you don't care,
       so I won't too,

As the cop down the hall watches
          me watch
You shoot up.

Jesus and Moses,
       anything you wanna bring
           down . . .

I'll bring
            a lawyer . . . I don't know
                        what I did...
I must've been bad...they throw words at you . . .

Now dig what I added to the thing. . . .

If I could reach you
            from my cell, I'd roll
                        up your sleeve

And wrap the rubber band
            tourniquetly.

I'd slide the needle toward the slowest of motions—

Habit and prayer.

Do it.

This whole generation's strung out.

We can't do it
            all on our own.

My period's a semi-colon now,
            the days get longer and longer.

Shhh.

You're elliptical, safe, clear.

You should see
            what your smile looks like
                        from here.

Still Life with Addict

He's way too stoned. Again. It's cold out there,
But there he is, a left, a right, Ali,
Or Cassius Clay, the shadow. *Fuck you, boy.*
I'll drop your ass, rag-ass mother-fucker.
There's no one there, but there he swings, then holds
His index finger up so all take heed
To all he can't not say. He's gone. The crack,
Or angel dust, or methamphetamine—
The names don't seem to matter much. It's all
The same rush that puts his past right inside
My ear. And now I hear the future. *What?*
You gonna what? I dare you. No one there,
Except for Clay, Ali. They're not the same.
Ain't got no heart. I'm the one with heart, bitch.
Shit. Drop your ass in one, two, Rope-a-Dope.
He has a voice. He has two hands. He floors
The air with three hard blows, and then falls down.
His breath is white and crystalled. The still life
Is in the breath, how it hangs there, freezing.
He stands up, kissing his blood-cracked knuckles.

Malcolm X Transcribing the Dictionary in Slow Motion

The dictionary contains the only sentence that never ends

And for you Malcolm I offer one that does

But takes its time and catches its breath
                                        stretching

Its lines as far as the margin that is the end

Of the world and so begins again
                                        knowing

How the beginning is the end that waits blankly

Knowing it can never be shaken
                                        delayed

The All-Knowing End of Things

Where the soul comes from
                                        toward where it returns

The beginning again because you don't know

Which words you need to learn

You take your time and you do your time

You live your sentence and you live your sentence out

Clear your throat and lick
                                        the pencil's tip

Turn the page and fill your tablets up
                        and by ten p.m. each night

You rage against the dying lights

Turn inward
           the closest kind of reading
Where words are empty and real

But only at the end
               as the sun rises
                      and the moon fades

And sparrows bathe in a puddle of dust

Because they must
              because it feels it just

So

Still Life with You

Men who mean just what they say . . .
                    —"The Ballad of the Green Berets"

Imagination was a killer.
                    —Tim O'Brien, "The Things They Carried"

And it's still true,

There may always be a certain darkness that descends
Behind the eyes, always a certain silence

That rises inside the lungs;

It's true.

When the two come together,
A momentary clarity, as wide as wind,

Overtakes the body, something beyond eternity, beyond
Any memory of eternity, beyond staring

At the blankness this page offers:

You, this elegy-in-waiting,
You, this ghost-written-self-portrait,
You, this still-life-fidgeting, craving its next fix. . . .

You see,

* * *

The most important thing I've learned about growing up
In Sharon Hill was calling him

Chicken Man while trying to imagine
His brief tour in Vietnam, and how

His life seemed to end, but drag
Each day from then on because of those four months.

(One day, sitting under a banyan tree,

His mind flickered, and he saw all
                                    that could never be seen.)

Each day, waiting for the bus, I'd watch him unravel
A piece of tinfoil that held little crystals

Of eternity, which seemed to make him
Distant, happier.

His eyes would water, then shine

Like high-rise windows,
The workers on ropes floating

Spider-like, while those behind the windows,
At their desks, stare, mesmerized

With the grace in which a body can rise or fall.

All that behind Chicken Man's eyes, it's true.

I can say that

Because once, he caught me staring
At him as he stepped into that other world

Where Vietnam might have been a goose-down comforter,

And Southern Comfort rain,
Rain a God-blown golden light,

That light a king-sized bed called the world,
A palimpsest for the one we're in right now,

Where memory, I'm thinking, could have been scraped
Clean for him, darkness and silence extinct,

Where facts bleed through
                              whatever the truth wants

To be.

Fact is, when our eyes locked,
His nostrils flared and his pupils filled

With actual bright matter, and he held out
His arms and turned up his palms, Christ-like.

Offering his throat to the clouds, he pointed
Right at me:

You . . .

Truth is, it was those ellipses that rippled
Down my spine, all he left unsaid, and meant,

Dark and silent.

I was 15.

Would you like me to say
                              that in that moment I understood

What darkness and silence were,

That I could taste them as I would my own
Breath blown into my lungs

For the first time?

Or would you prefer to see a green path
Canopied with small palms, banyans, bamboos, liana vines,

An entire forest as still as a bible;

And on one side of that path, a patrol unit:
Some of them napping,

Some writing home, one sharpening a knife, another
Listening, not for Charlie, but to the trees,

And to the golden-winged laughing thrushes
And plain white storks sleeping inside them?

Do you think Chicken Man wouldn't be writing home,
To Sharon Hill, not then,

When he still had a home?

You're right, and it's true: Chicken Man,
The story has it, enlisted, still suffering

From a belief in the old lie: a difference
Between right and wrong.

The longer he listened, the more he heard
Silence and darkness growing. At first,

It was a gentle rustle, a little wind in the vines,
As if someone were turning Revelation's pages; then,

A thrush ruffled its feathers, a little more wind,
Another thrush called something out,

And another responded, and the wind rose
And the sun set and the sun rose again,

And Chicken Man sat there listening.

By morning, his unit had begun watching him, whispering
To each other, cracking jokes until there was nothing

More for them to joke about, and they grew
Quiet, listening to Chicken Man's listening.

When the sergeant called out to him,
Chicken Man rose slowly, deliberately, as if

He were at Mass,

And emptied his M-16 assault rifle into the men.

When each man fell, he murmured you,
Seven times in all. Then, he sat back down

And waited for the thrushes to begin again.

You and *you* and *you* and *you* and *you* and *you* and *you*...
Each you higher in pitch, until one

Could've believed he was responding
To the thrushes' calls.

If something in his mind flickered, a tinge
Of regret maybe, then this is no longer a true story.

If all he wanted was to listen to birds sing
And wind wind its way through vines,

Then this has something to do with you.

I have to believe
              he didn't mean what he did,

Only what he said.

He was a long way from home, from Sharon Hill,
Where the most important thing

Is saying exactly what you mean.

IV

Still Life with Geraniums

—for my grandmothers

The blood orange sky began to nestle
Its way inside your winter geraniums

Weeks ago, a gathering of hands
Hammered by light, water, and care disguised

As a loss I want to explain away.

A flower is burial, nothing more

Than a reanimation of your hands
I might have glimpsed just now inside this last,

Or next-to-last, still life. I could say it

Was wind, someone else's imagination
Taking over, yours perhaps, and you might

Tell me that the petals shiver a little
As you shift dirt so roots open and breathe.

You might try to wipe the sweat from your eyes,

And when you look up, you find the sun just
Where you thought it would be, the sting strong

Enough to slow the light that wants to take
Us elsewhere, back to where we began,

Which is why we will not explain the need

To look up at this, our, blood orange sky

While the geraniums begin to swell.

Ars Poetica #17

Look, my grandmothers would float out
Of themselves and into me nearly
Every day the weeks after they died.
I'd find myself pickling eggs,
Making a pot roast, polishing
Silver spoons and china, caring.
Once, I stole tomatoes right off
The Maltese's vines. I wanted
Something fresh for once. I hate tomatoes,
And the Maltese's are my neighbors,
Friends of the family, which must be why
They told me they saw the whole thing,
And laughed, and felt "a little sad."
"My losses and all," someone said.
Yes, my grandmothers floated out
Of themselves and into me, and in
The mirror one morning, I saw them
And felt me. They must've loved me,
I guess. Why else would they keep showing
Up as me, in me, to me?
                    Here
Is where I feel my face changing,
My voice turning strangely fainter,
Trailing because…I don't know why,
Why elegies bore me, why grandmothers
In poems bore me, great poems praising
The dead bore me. The dead put me
To sleep while they write, then read, this poem.
Why should I complain? I am happy
Now, which must be why all I want
To write from now on should begin
With the dead listening
                    again.

Still Life with the Atlantic Ocean
and Nina Simone as Soundtrack

Wave and gull lament the same soul
Because they share it, just like the rest of us.

They sing its loss,
And so claim its permanence

Before it's even born,

Especially in March, in Atlantic City,
When it's easier to walk the untouched sand, graying

While another spring closes in.

You, too, might try to add a little to the song,

You might sing as loudly as you can
The chorus from Brel's "Ne Me Quitte Pas" to no one,

You'll spread your arms and clench your fists
Not unlike Nina Simone,

Who one night, on stage, actually broke
Down right before the end of the last verse:

Laisse-moi devenir
L'ombre de ton ombre
L'ombre de ta main. . . .

Her grief was so violent she shook.

When the bass player tried to help her
Off stage, she broke his nose,

Not over some unresolved squabble about who
Got paid what, but over who he was not—

Her husband, who had filed for divorce that afternoon.

Those at the club who knew the song
Couldn't have caught the irony, the inevitable clash

Between memory and grief—
Which is not a clash at all—

Because they didn't know the story.

Nor is there anything ironic, now, to speak of.

All you hear is a still life trying to scratch its way
Out of a lament for itself,
                              what Simone could not sing

That night, from what the crowd expected
To hear, but didn't; or if they did,

They hummed it to themselves as they walked home,
Relieved, more than anything,

Not to be Ms. Simone.

The point of this story is that you're alone,
That everything ends up pretty OK, a little

Memory inside the grief, a little silence inside
The dark, a little motion inside memory

So you might feel the Atlantic
Throw its blue riff through your ribs

And try to finish the song,
Answering to no one.

You don't even have to sound good.

All you need to do is believe

That, in this moment,
Stillness is the illusion that goes on and on,

That the Atlantic's grief and Simone's grief
Are parts of the same illusion that always fall

Into the design of a wave that refuses to break.

That's the way it's always been, right?

Some illusion, like this salt air

That holds your parents now, long before they disappeared,

As far back as any beginning goes, further than 1972,
When a climax became your name;

The night your parents, after a bottle Pinot Noir
And a little Nina Simone on vinyl,

Did their best to destroy time
And ended up with you,

You beginning somewhere,
                              say Atlantic City,

With an ocean view and ocean sounds,
                                        ocean rhythms,

All that motion fluid, explosive, distinct,
Never slow enough.

You have to live with that fact, just
Like everyone else,
                    sort of.

What lures you, anyone, back to stillness, finally,
Is a need to know some things

That couldn't be any less personal

Than a waterfall:

That recording of Simone, for example, her purring
On the phonograph, her refusal to give in

To the stillness that finally overtook her,

When she actually did finish the song, years before
The breakup,
                in the studio,

Her husband behind the soundproof glass, staring,
In awe of her,

Saying something like *take a break*,
Or *keep that one*, or *how do you do*

That...?

It must've seemed important to her,

To know what he said,
                        and why she never asked

Him.

Spilt Coffee in Slow Motion

Los doce. Vamos a la cintura del día.
—Vallejo

Say I can't tell you yet.
Say it's a simple matter
Of tenses getting tangled,

Letting go, and scattering
Like solitude, and rain, and roads.
Or say it's not so

Simple: a car accident
On a city corner. Sad,
Really, how personal things become

At the end. The collision happened
Before any of us have been born,
A Wednesday, noon, late

June blue filling the sky,
None of us yet in a place
We'll never be able to leave,

None of us offering anything
Distinct about childhood,
None of us much caring until much later.

Say the police set up a makeshift triage,
A cop with his hand
On a woman's shoulder.

Say someone gives
Her some coffee, and she holds it
Loosely, an indifference

Mixed with dependence
In her posture, as if she
Needs something less

Than she knows. Childhood
Will do that, sometimes seconds
Before your sedan slams a van

Full of next year's phonebooks
And sends the driver through
The windshield and into a body

Cast for two months.
Truth is, it happened years
Ago or it hasn't happened yet.

But I have stand here listening
To those Bible-thin pages
Turning in a summer breeze.

It feels . . . nice.
Then another collision will happen:
The woman with the coffee,

I will hear her again.
She'll slap the cop's back,
Will keep slapping and keep

Saying who who who,
And she won't ever stop.
The lid on her cup will snap off.

She'll look as if she's dancing.
She'll look up at the sky,
And will feel that burn called loss,

And we'll watch it spill down her
Arm and skirt, like a memory
That exiles each of us

From this afternoon
And scatters us onto a page
As blank as childhood's,

Slow and short as it is.

Goodbye in Slow Motion with Those Trees Waving Back

As if these words could alter wind's lucid course
And make the trees wave hello again;

As if the wind had something new to bless,
Confess; that, finally, today's losses were palpable, explicable

Even; as if there were a reason for this self-pity
To descend again like shade

From the maples and lilacs and palms,
The sweet peach and lacquered locust,

Those cherries, chestnuts, and oranges. . . . It has to be

All of them, all of them
                    lining those streets whose names I loved:

Calle de la Bonanova, Rue Descartes, Aldstadter Ring,
And further still, Coates and Sharon, which aren't

In Barcelona, Paris, or Prague, but from Sharon Hill, from
    childhood,
Places that don't exist anymore.

As if childhood were some tourist destination to visit
Off season, walking those sun-stroked sidewalks,

Sipping wine in the street-side cafés, saying hello to those
I'll never know in a tongue I used to know.

As if anyone's history were myth, and that myth an
    unconditional love
For loss. As if sorry didn't exist,

Any need for sorry.

If only childhood would tell the wind where to go,
If only it had a home.

If only this poem could hold childhood in its hands—
All gnarl-knuckled, chapped, blood-cracked—long enough

To say goodbye, to the bartender in Prague
Who was from Brooklyn, who talked with me awhile

About what home can't mean to him anymore, who got lost
Hiking in the Alpines and "ended up in here somehow, never
    left. . . ."

As if childhood's a place never left and never found, never
Said goodbye to;

As if that mattered now, as if there were time enough
To say goodbye to childhood

With all the slowness loss demands;

As if loss and childhood were distinct.

As if there were someone to talk with, walk and smoke with.

Besides, after awhile, we'd feel a need to sleep,
This me and that you I once was,

Our skin chilled a little, turning to gooseflesh a little, swept
By an August breeze weaving its way through the trees.

It doesn't matter, though, does it?
You've already begun to name the trees for yourself.

But feel that?

The trees are waving, too.

I'd like to teach you the names of these trees, to confess
How much I need to miss you to finish this off.

v

Still Life with a Grain of Rice

I used to like the way things went together:

Chopin and Auden; apocalypse and abyss;
Given and give in; disgust

And discussed. Chopin's

"No. 3 in B major," at the end,
For instance, how he reaches

As far as he can across the piano
With both arms—as if hearing himself

For the first time—

Like Icarus, maybe.

I used to think I'd love
To plunge like that

And be done with it.

There must be something
In me that refuses

To die, I pray.

But, Auden's Icarus stares down
At the indifferent ploughman and all

His shares he needs to live on,
Which make his lord richer

Forever.

If I were there, in that Brueghel,
I'd turn away, too, from something

Amazing—a boy falling
Out of the sky—because I did,

In fact, do it.

Early September in a new millennium,
And I had nowhere to get to.

I wasn't in New York yet.

A gorgeous day:
The sun shone

On the television,
Through the high windows

Of my bedroom where
I confessed an important failure

To no one:

Don't look, don't care.

I was eating a bowl of rice
With teriyaki steak

For breakfast.

I licked the white fork clean
And wanted more

While someone fell out of the sky
For real.

And then another.

I turned up Chopin and licked
A grain of rice I'll never

Write a poem on

Now.

All I've wanted since is to sail
Calmly on.

And I do,

Letting the dead down.

Still Life with Birch Trees in Minsk and a Portrait of Pushkin

Before I left,
I spent a month's worth of mornings

Watching these birches

Bend in the summer winds
Of Minsk.

Sometimes the gusts were strong
Enough to hurt them

Into right angles

Before they returned
To a perfect verticality

Entirely their own.

They never slouched,
Even in their old age, and refused to break.

Their calm complaints hung in the air
Like the inevitable music

Of waves crashing,
Or traffic on a highway heard from a hill.

It's ridiculous, admissions
Like these, but I came to love

These trees that die
So swiftly by the hand of a man

Who really needs them

To boil some water
That'll make some soup

Or clean a shirt.

* * *

If trees have families, then entire generations
Are hacked to a death as well,

A death that's paid for

By a group of men in suits that shine
If you catch them

In a certain light, men
Who decide when it's time to clear the land

For casinos appearing along the lakes
Just outside the center of this city

I was just beginning to love
Before I was forced to leave it.

Memory blurs and softens,
Especially in the present tense,

The tense of miracles,

The only tense trees possess,

Certain of their greatness,

Certain of their desire
To be nothing greater.

* * *

This is the magnificent lie
I began to believe

As I walked, slowly, most afternoons
Through The Great Patriotic War Museum,

Which is not much more than a basement
Floor of an office building controlled by the State,

And contains photographs that should never be shown
To children and adults,

And need to be seen
As long as the banners

Of hatred wave indifferently
In this world.

I experienced my own hatred
As I stared at a painting

Of Pushkin stabbed three times
By bayonets of Nazi soldiers:

Once for being a Communist, once
For being black, and once

For being a poet.

Maybe those soldiers were beyond fatigue and were certain
The painting was a man alive,

His right eyebrow dipping, maybe
In speculation, maybe in condemnation,

His lips moist, pursed, beginning
A curse or conjuring some spit,

And so judging them.

Or not.

It's hard to say
Which would be worse.

Maybe it was their souls
That compelled them to stab

The canvas, just to feel something certain:

Vandalizing an otherwise unremarkable portrait
Of an irreplaceable poet

Lacking tension,

Before that war, anyway.

* * *

Memory blurs and softens, and context
Sires tragedy, and then certainty.

It's an old story.

The soldiers were boys.

Pushkin had been dead over a hundred years,

And if those Nazi soldiers felt something
More real than ideology

As they stabbed a portrait,

Well, maybe they did. Of that,
At least, they were certain,

Before they froze to death.

                    * * *

But, if there are gods,

They must look down on us
The way trees do

As they track a fire
That'll consume them soon enough,

A fire that seems as though it will never have enough

Air.

And if trees are gods, their stare is certain
In its indifference.

It looks like air,
But feels like fire

On the flesh, a fact

That's always puzzled them,

Having flesh so unlike ours.

                    * * *

Fuck it, I said to myself
As I was held up

At Customs, as the agents refused
To let me through

To what I was certain was my right,
My home, an America I loathed

And needed,

As I offered a pack of Marlboro Reds
And a fifth of Glenlivet 12,

As if those would get it all back,

As if petty vices offer passage
And bring anyone closer

To whatever's home.

As if any vice were petty.

Fuck it, I said, and sat
In the little room

With no windows.

* * *

Birches
Have listened to their own groans

For so long
They must recite them

In every tongue
No human

Could ever understand.

This, I'm certain, is what I heard
Those mornings in Minsk

Before I was told to leave.

It must be maddening, withstanding
Something inevitable, essential:

A wind

That makes a tree
Appear as though it's ashamed of itself,

As it continues rising

Despite and because

Of it.

Still Life with Hikmet Sailing toward Stalingrad, Not Listening to The Beach Boys

It's not impossible. That much
I know, for this is

One of the only lives to be

Had, and the Truth's a wooden match
That could light his cigarette

I'd throw overboard or to the wind

As Brian Wilson is living

Out the hell of days that'll become his
Childhood, which will give birth

To the chorus and hook

Of "Sloop John B."

It's possible, too, that

There are lies we tell
And lies we must believe

If we'll ever make Time

Turn on its heels and walk
Like the derelict it is

With its hands in its pockets,
Half turning back

After catching our stare,

And struck with that fear it knows
All too well,

Quickens its pace, ducks left,
And disappears.

Lying like this is the only way
I can make myself believe

That I'm here,

On this ship in 1951 while Stalin grins
In his sleep

And McCarthy greases
His comb over before descending

The steps of the Senate Floor.

I might be invisible, I might be
A fellow Turkish Exile, I might even be

In the shape of me that's here and now
Writing this all down

For Hikmet and to Hikmet

As I take out my iPod and scroll
Until I find The Beach Boys' only song

I've got, the one that's made me
Cry, thankfully,

To no one.

It's the purity, the majesty,

It's hook and chorus—I wanna go home—the beauty
Of its impossibility,

The immutable in each of us:

Exile,

An epiphany so stale
Hikmet snuffs out the cigarette

He's only half smoked.

His stare is water
At every temperature.

His anger

Couldn't resemble Heaven less.

He's beyond calm, beyond
Music, he is

No longer

Himself,
              devastated,

Wrapped in a Soviet brown blanket.

He looks at me
As if I were a distant relative,

And spits. He breathes
Into his hands

And leans back into his chair.

The ship muscles its way
Through frozen ocean

That will turn into Stalingrad
And exile

And a heart attack

As the stars clarify,

As Wilson sings,

As Hikmet's stare remains
Fixed,

Like the future.

Still Life with Issa at the Gates

Let's go
To a place where no one waits

Instead

Let's say we have a choice
Where there are no centuries

Let's say we make a new line inside

The heavens inside the veins
Inside the salts inside the oceans'

Air giving way
To a place where nothing makes us free

Where God bows
                blushes and bows

Before His children

Call that Heaven

No smoke no flesh
Falling heavily

With rain and names and hands
And sun and eyes

As strong as smoke
And childhood
            and holocaust

That still life
          instead

Still
     God
          another myth goes

Had to die once too
And prayed enough

Ahead of time

What myth loves you
                    back

I like Issa's for its eternity

Its stillness

And yet . . .
And yet . . .

Still Life with a Field Mouse
and Adolf Eichmann in Buenos Aires

Maybe it's through the iris of a field mouse
Where the afterlife opens

And prayers end,

The dark and blank

Iris of a field mouse.

Another impossibility,
Another trace

Of God's humanity,
That's all.

Another perpetual image,
Another failed essence.

* * *

I knew it was a field mouse when I held it up
To the light

In my kitchen by its tail, my three cats circling
Me, reaching for it

The way, I guess, any of us

Would reach for something
Without guilt. I wish

I could end the poem here
With the field mouse staring back at me, still

Alive, thanking me, maybe, through its stare
And its forced complicity to simply hang

There until I took it outside.

Alive, the field mouse conjures the still life
I'm trying to write

Because instinct told my cats what to do,
And so they bowed, shimmied, and struck.

When I stomped my foot, my upstairs
Neighbor's shelves shook

And my cats scattered, and hid,
And waited.

* * *

Not knowing what else to do,
I wrapped the field mouse in a paper towel

And carried it outside, to a place
That too much resembled it,

Grayer than winter and thinner than wind,

Then cupped it in my hand
For what felt like a time long enough

For such a death
To mean something.

Wrapped in a paper towel,
It weighed as much as a paper towel.

I placed it on the curb,
Went back inside, and cracked

Open a bottle of beer.
I lit a cigarette, and tried to finish the book

Of Holocaust poetry I was reading.

I tried to understand it all, again,
And failing again, found myself

Staring at smoke rising
From my mouth into a dim light.

The rest of my cigarette burned itself away
As I watched from my kitchen window

Street-sweeper trucks drift
Like a flock of stars.

One of the drivers leaned out his side door
And waved at someone

Only he must've seen.

* * *

Come dawn, not having slept,
I went out to the curb to see

If I'd done right by a field mouse

Killed in my home.

All that was left
Was a tuft from its back,

No bigger than a clot
Of blood Adolf Eichmann might have spat up

Each morning for ten years
In Buenos Aires.

The crows and the water-logged wind
Of winter,

Each had played a part,
Did what needed to be done, not knowing

Why God wouldn't be
Found in the details.

Not caring, either. Not
Having to.

                        *   *   *

Instinct is the true God.

A field mouse killed like this,
And who cares? A poet

Once put it directly: "Me. I do. It's mine."

There's only one way, I guess,
To address the dark,

Especially when it's tucked within

The smallest of places, the iris
Of a field mouse or the dollop of air

Beneath a cat's tongue or the hole in the sky
A star has failed to fill,

And because I found that field mouse, because
I was the last living thing it saw,

I have to pray. I don't want to
Pray, and now I have to:

Poor cats,
Pray for us.

Poorer still, crows,
Pray for us.

Poorest of all,
You, field mouse, will you pray for us

As the American housewife, exiled in her own country
And body, shoos your shadow away,

As she stands shrieking on a chair in her own kitchen

In those racist cartoons of my childhood
With a housemaid in a red bandana

Drawn too tightly around her head?

Poor Tom & Jerry, and Hannah & Barbera,
Warner Bros., Hollywood,

America and its peculiar institutions,

Pray for us.

Poor Sweet Homes of Everywhere, pray for us.

Poor Argentina with its fingerprints
Of Ricardo Klement woven into its national fabric,

Pray for us.

Poor Ricardo Klement, who ever he may be,
Never Adolf Eichmann, really,

Pray for us.

Pray for us, Poor History after Auschwitz and everything
After and after and before,

Where Eichmann can become anyone,

Where wind sways equally the maple and lilac and palm,
The locust and orange,

The pine and cherry and chestnut,
The oak and maple and birch,

Its music a language

No one's truly mastered
By the end.

Poor instinct, poor belief, poor fear,
Pray for us,

Your children.

Poor abstractions, how little you carry
From our prayers into our lives,

Pray for us.

How much was promised back then.

And, you, Afterlife, composed as you are

In an iris

Blank and dark, belonging as equally
To a field mouse as it might

To an Eichmann,

Poor thing, trying so earnestly
To find yourself

In a bit of dark at first,
Then a little more, and more, and more

Until your image, this shattered still life,
Is held against

What's unignorable:

What's to be done for you?

Notes

PAGE 20, "STILL LIFE WITH FREDERICK DOUGLASS LEARNING THE ALPHABET, STOPPING FOR A MOMENT AT O": The impetus for this poem came not only from Frederick Douglass' well-known memoir *A Narrative of the Life of Frederick Douglass, an American Slave* but also from his second (and lesser known) memoir, *My Bondage, My Freedom.* The poem didn't fully reveal itself to me, however, until I reread Audre Lord, specifically "Sister Outsider," in which she says, "The true focus of revolutionary change is never merely the oppressive situations which we seek to escape, but that piece of the oppressor which is planted deep within each of us."

PAGE 23, "FLASH FORWARD WITH THE AMISTAD BEFORE US IN THE DISTANCE": The Amistad case is perhaps the most genuinely American narrative we have. I wrote this poem years before I learned of Kevin Young's book *Ardency: A Chronicle of The Amistad Rebels.* I have written only, so far, one poem on this topic. Young has written a book. Consult his book. It is history, and it is art. In short, it's poetry.

PAGE 24, "STILL LIFE WITH SISYPHUS SMILING": The epigraph is taken from Albert Camus' essay "The Myth of Sisyphus."

PAGE 27, "STILL LIFE WITH PAUL CELAN BY THE SEINE": Celan, 1920–1970, was a German-speaking Jew born in a section then known as Romania and what's known today as Ukraine. In 1942, his parents were rounded up in a Nazi pogrom and were killed either in or en route to a concentration camp in Transnistria. After World War II, he eventually settled in Paris. On April 20, 1970, he drowned himself in the Seine. He is one of our most necessary twentieth-century poets.

PAGE 35, "REVELATION IN SLOW MOTION": Hannah Arendt's extraordinary book *Eichmann in Jerusalem: A Report on the Banality of*

Evil helped me finish this poem, but I don't think it can ever be finished. I wonder, too, if I should have ever started it.

PAGE 55, "STILL LIFE WITH LENNY BRUCE IN JAIL": American comedian Lenny Bruce was first arrested in 1961 in San Francisco on obscenity charges for saying the words "cocksucker" and "come." Later that year, he was arrested in Philadelphia on drug charges. In 1964, he was arrested after a show in Greenwich Village on specious grounds by undercover police in the audience who later testified that they genuinely enjoyed the show. This poem visits Bruce in any of those jail cells. Bruce died of an "accidental overdose of morphine" in 1966. He was granted a posthumous pardon in 2003 by New York Governor George Pataki.

PAGE 58, "MALCOLM X TRANSCRIBING THE DICTIONARY IN SLOW MOTION": In his autobiography, Malcolm X claims to have transcribed the dictionary in longhand. I believe him.

PAGE 95, "STILL LIFE WITH HIKMET SAILING TOWARD STALINGRAD, NOT LISTENING TO THE BEACH BOYS": Nazim Hikmet, 1902–1963, was a Turkish poet who spent almost his entire adult life either in prison or in exile because of his outspoken Communist beliefs. In 1950, while in prison, he was awarded the International Peace Prize along with Picasso, Neruda, Robeson, and Jakubowska. He eventually escaped from Turkey and emigrated to Russia, where, in 1963, he died of a heart attack. Despite the systematic persecution he endured from the Turkish regime, Hikmet never lost his love for his country and its people.

PAGE 99, "STILL LIFE WITH ISSA AT THE GATES": The last lines of this poem are Issa's via Robert Hass's translation, which can be found in *The Essential Haiku*.

PAGE 101, "STILL LIFE WITH A FIELD MOUSE AND ADOLF EICHMANN IN BUENOS AIRES": From 1950 to 1960, Adolf Eichmann, his wife, and children lived under a stolen identity in Buenos Aires. With assistance from various international agencies, Eichmann appropriated the identity of Ricardo Klement. If Eichmann spat up blood every morning for ten years . . . I don't know. It brings me no pleasure to imagine whether he did or didn't. History, however, hasn't given me a choice.

About the Author

Alexander Long's books include *Vigil* (New Issues Poetry & Prose, 2006) and *Light Here, Light There* (C & R Press, 2009). A chapbook, also titled *Still Life*, was selected for the 2010 Center for Book Arts Chapbook Competition. With Christopher Buckley, Long is the co-editor of *A Condition of the Spirit: The Life & Work of Larry Levis* (Eastern Washington UP, 2004). Originally from Sharon Hill, Pennsylvania, he lives in Hoboken with his wife Marina Fedosik-Long and three cats.

The White Pine Press Poetry Prize

Vol. 16 *Still Life* by Alexander Long. Selected by Aliki Barnstone

Vol. 15 *Letters From the Emily Dickinson Room* by Kelli Russell Agodon. Selected by Carl Dennis

Vol. 14 *In Advance of All Parting* by Ansie Baird. Selected by Roo Borson

Vol. 13 *Ghost Alphabet* by Al Maginnes. Selected by Peter Johnson

Vol. 12 *Paper Pavilion* by Jennifer Kwon Dobbs. Selected by Genie Zeiger

Vol. 11 *The Trouble with a Short Horse in Montana* by Roy Bentley. Selected by John Brandi

Vol. 10 *The Precarious Rhetoric of Angels* by George Looney. Selected by Nin Andrews

Vol. 9 *The Burning Point* by Frances Richey. Selected by Stephen Corey

Vol. 8 *Watching Cartoons Before Attending a Funeral* by John Surowiecki. Selected by C.D. Wright

Vol. 7 *My Father Sings, To My Embarrassment* by Sandra Castillo. Selected by Cornelius Eady

Vol. 6 *If Not For These Wrinkles of Darkness* by Stephen Frech. Selected by Pattiann Rogers

Vol. 5 *Trouble in History* by David Keller. Selected by Pablo Medina

Vol. 4 *Winged Insects* by Joel Long. Selected by Jane Hirshfield

Vol. 3 *A Gathering of Mother Tongues* by Jacqueline Joan Johnson. Selected by Maurice Kenny

Vol. 2 *Bodily Course* by Deborah Gorlin. Selected by Mekeel McBride

Vol. 1 *Zoo & Cathedral* by Nancy Johnson. Selected by David St. John

ACKNOWLEDGMENTS (continued)

Thanks to Aliki Barnstone for believing in these poems.

A chapbook containing eight of these poems, also titled *Still Life*, was printed by the Center for Book Arts in New York City. Thanks to Terrance Hayes and Sharon Dolin for selecting those poems. Thanks to Barbara Henry for making a beautiful book.

Thanks to Christopher Buckley, Kate Northrop, Beth Bachmann, Philip Levine, Fleda Brown, William Olsen, Curtis Bauer, Sebastian Matthews, Elaine Sexton, and Ross Gay; as well as Luke Stromberg, Elisabeth Majewski, Luke Bauerlein, Christina Vogt-Hennessey, Zachary Burkhart, Stephanie Lawrence, Matt Thomas, Dorothy von Gerbig, Katrina Rutt-Hayes, and Matt Hayes.

Thanks to my colleagues at John Jay College, especially Devin Harner, Paul Narkunas, P. J. Gibson, Adam Berlin, Margaret Mikesell-Tabb, Jeffrey Heiman, Richard Haw, Sanjana Nair, and Toy-Fung Tung.

Thanks to my colleagues in the City University of New York's Faculty Fellowship Publication Program: Bridgette Davis, Ava Chin, Carlos Hernandez, Racquel Goodison, Alisa Roost, and Johannah Rodgers.

Thanks, always, to my family for their unswerving support.

Thanks, always, to Marina for her honesty, encouragement, and being.